I0816474

AMAZING OCEAN LIFE

Sea Turtles

by Colleen Sexton

Kaleidoscope
Minneapolis, MN

Where the Quest for Discovery Begins

This edition first published in 2023 by Kaleidoscope Publishing, Inc.

Kaleidoscope Publishing, Inc.
6012 Blue Circle Drive
Minnetonka, MN 55343

Library of Congress Control Number
2022937425

ISBN
978-1-64519-565-8 (library bound)
978-1-64519-635-8 (ebook)

Bigfoot Jr. lurks within one of the images in this book. It's up to you to find him!

Table of Contents

Underwater Swimmers

Whoosh! A sea turtle slowly swims through ocean waters.

Sea turtles are **reptiles**. They have lived on Earth for more than 200 million years.

olive ridley

loggerhead

leatherback

flatback

green

Kemp's ridley

hawksbill

There are seven different kinds of sea turtles.

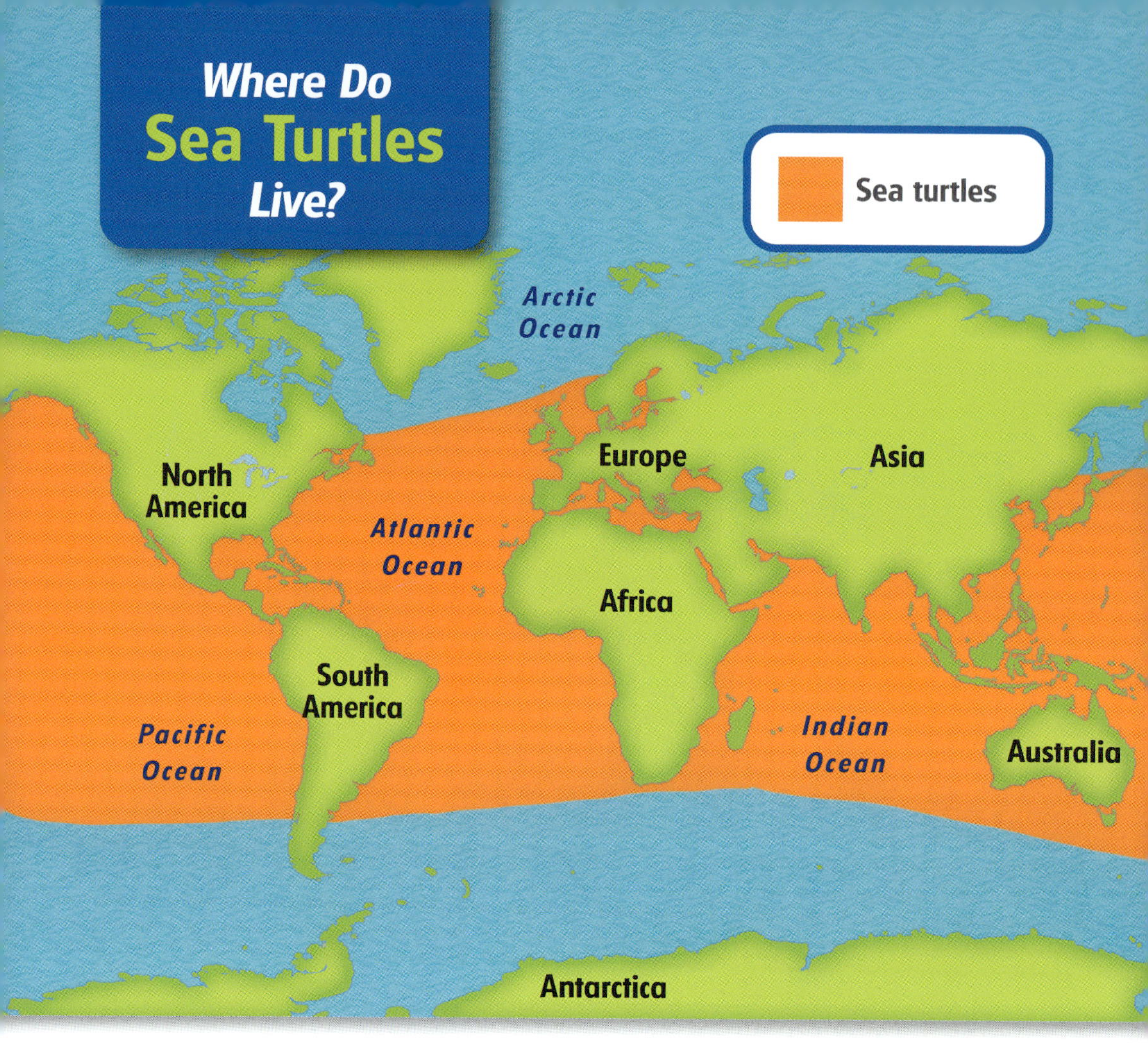

Sea turtles are found in oceans around the world.

Most sea turtles live in warm waters close to shore. Some swim near **coral reefs**. Some live where rivers meet the ocean.

Shells and Scales

A sea turtle's head has strong jaws and a sharp **beak**.

A sea turtle has a hard, bony shell. The shell's flat shape helps the sea turtle slide through water.

A sea turtle has scaly skin. Large **scales** called scutes cover the sea turtle's top shell.

A sea turtle has four **flippers**. It uses the front flippers to paddle forward. It uses the back flippers to turn and stop.

Parts of a Sea Turtle

Diving for Dinner

A sea turtle searches for a good place to feed. Sometimes it must swim far to find one.

Sea turtles eat both plants and animals. Some of their favorites are seaweed, fish, crabs, and jellyfish.

The sea turtle takes a breath and dives. It can see and smell **prey** deep underwater.

The sea turtle catches its prey! It bites the prey with its beak and sucks it into its mouth. *Gulp!*

What Eats
Sea Turtles?

Baby Sea Turtles

Female sea turtles leave their feeding places. They **migrate** to the beach where they will lay their eggs.

At night, the female sea turtle drags her heavy body onto shore. She crawls up the beach.

FUN FACT

A female sea turtle goes back to the beach where she hatched to lay her eggs.

The female sea turtle makes a nest. She digs a hole in the sand with her flippers.

She lays about 100 round eggs in the nest. She covers them with sand. Then she crawls back to the ocean.

Baby sea turtles hatch about two months later. They dig out of the nest at night.

FUN FACT

Baby sea turtles have a sharp egg tooth. They use it to break out of their shells.

The baby sea turtles rush down the beach. They reach the water. The waves carry them out to sea.

Photo Glossary

beak: A hard, pointed mouth. A sea turtle has a sharp beak.

coral reef: A form of rock made of old and new corals. Many animals that sea turtles hunt live on coral reefs.

flippers: Flat arms that some ocean animals use to swim. A sea turtle has four flippers.

migrate: To move from one place to another. Some sea turtles migrate more than 1,000 miles (1,600 kilometers) to nest.

prey: An animal that is hunted by another animal for food. A sea turtle can see and smell prey deep underwater.

reptile: A cold-blooded animal with a backbone that lays eggs to produce young. Sea turtles are reptiles.

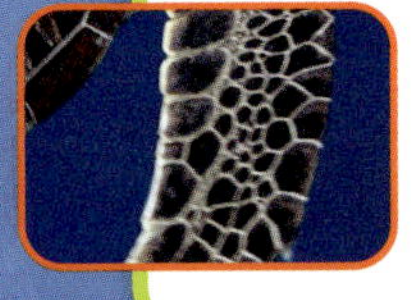

scale: A piece of hard skin covering a reptile's body. Large scales cover the sea turtle's top shell.

Read More

Esbaum, Jill. *Sea Turtles.* Go Wild! Washington, DC: National Geographic Kids, 2021.

Grack, Rachel. *Sea Turtles.* Animals at Risk. Minneapolis, MN: Bellwether Media, 2022.

Zommer, Yuval. *The Big Book of the Blue.* New York, NY: Thames & Hudson, 2018.

Factsurfer.com gives you a safe, fun way to find more information.

1. Go to www.factsurfer.com.
2. Enter “Sea Turtles” into the search box and click 🔍
3. Select your book cover to see a list of related websites.

About the Author

Colleen Sexton is a writer and editor. She is the author of more than one hundred nonfiction books for kids on topics ranging from astronauts to glaciers to elephants. She lives in Minnesota.

INDEX

PHOTO CREDITS

The images in this book are reproduced through Shutterstock: EA Given 1, 10-11; Rich Carey 3; Shane Myers Photography 5; David Carbo 6; Ekaterina Kuzmenkova 7; David Carbo 8; aquapix 8, 22; icestylecg 9; PUMPZA 10; saber photography 12, 22; Chai Seamaker 13; olias32 13; Lotus Images 13; Yana Georgieva 13; Chai Seamaker 14; Nerthuz 15; Mike Price 15; dangdumrong 15; Eric Isselee 15; Bandersnatch 16; David Evison 18; antpkr 19; IrinaK 20; kathayut kongmanee 21; bluefish_ds 21; Mekan Photography 22; Jirapong nontakanan 22; Happy monkey 22; Neophuket 22; Isabelle Kuehn 22; serg_dibrova 23. Cover: EA Given, Willyam Bradberry, Solarisys.